Editor
Eric Migliaccio

Managing Editor
Ina Massler Levin, M.A.

Editor-in-Chief
Sharon Coan, M.S. Ed.

Illustrator
Ben DeSoto

Cover Artist
Wendy Roy

Art Coordinator
Denice Adorno

Imaging
Rosa C. See

Product Manager
Phil Garcia

Publishers
Rachelle Cracchiolo, M.S. Ed.
Mary Dupuy Smith, M.S. Ed.

EVERYDAY WRITING

Grades 6-8

Written by

Susan Mackey Collins

Teacher Created Materials, Inc.
6421 Industry Way
Westminster, CA 92683
www.teachercreated.com

ISBN-0-7439-3615-9

© 2001 Teacher Created Materials, Inc.
Made in U.S.A.

Table of Contents

Introduction

Letters that were written long ago are fascinating. Part of the reason is, of course, the history that is revealed through the words of the writer. Also, though, there is a certain style to old letters. In today's hurried lifestyle, it is hard to imagine someone dipping his or her pen into a bottle of ink and setting the letters to paper that would later be sealed with dripping wax and the crest or insignia of the sender. Today, messages are sent instantly, fancy script is done by the touch of a computer key, and even the stationery comes pre-designed.

Help your students take pride in their writing by challenging them to think about the art of writing. *Everyday Writing* gives students practice in real-life writing. Students learn that there is a style and format that should be followed based on the writer's audience and purpose. By completing the activities in this book, students are taught that writing is both a learned skill and an art.

The following pages are filled with a wide variety of lessons and reproducible pages to be used with both middle- and high-school age students. The various lessons are designed to teach the technical writing skills that are required in many jobs and careers. The book is written to help students gain practice in such writing activities as filling out job applications, writing friendly letters and business letters, responding to newspaper advertisements, etc. The activities in this book also provide students with opportunities to practice skills that are required in the language-arts curriculum. By using the activities in this book, students gain understanding and development in writing, vocabulary, grammar, mechanics, and even public speaking skills.

The book includes practice in the following areas:

- ○ writing a friendly letter
- ○ writing a business letter
- ○ writing a thank you note
- ○ writing a bread and butter note
- ○ writing a letter of complaint
- ○ writing a business memo
- ○ using abbreviations in letter writing
- ○ addressing the envelope
- ○ completing applications and forms
- ○ using the correct tone

- ○ writing a resume
- ○ writing and sending e-mail
- ○ writing and sending a fax
- ○ writing messages
- ○ writing letters of advice
- ○ writing editorials
- ○ writing and following instructions
- ○ writing directions
- ○ writing for the classifieds
- ○ writing in today's high-tech society

Introduction *(cont.)*

There are several ways to use this book. Teachers may want to start at the beginning and continue straight through all of the lessons. This technique would be especially helpful for anyone teaching a "school to career" program or for teachers involved in units on technical writing.

Another way to use the activities is in conjunction with the school's guidance department. If a school participates in a career week, activities can be pulled from this book to help teach such useful skills as writing a business letter, completing an application or form, and writing a resume. These activities reinforce the skills that are emphasized during a schoolwide career program.

Everyday Writing is also an excellent source for educators wishing to teach computer skills in the language-arts classroom. Many of the activities are designed so students can complete the work with traditional pen and paper, but teachers wishing to emphasize the use of technology will find that many of the activities can be easily modified for this purpose.

For the teacher with only one computer in the classroom, the activities are written so that every student does not need to have access to a computer to complete the work. Teachers might choose to rotate computer time among the students, allowing some students to complete certain activities on the computer while others turn in a completed worksheet.

Also helpful are the Teacher Instruction pages and the Sample Lesson pages. The Teacher Instruction pages provide the teacher with helpful hints and ideas for teaching the lesson. The Sample Lesson pages are also helpful teaching tools and can be photocopied or made into overhead sheets.

No matter how the teacher decides to use the activities in this book, students will improve their writing skills. Students who complete the assignments will have a better understanding of the writing skills required in today's world.

The Parts of the Friendly Letter

The friendly letter is sometimes referred to as the social letter because the tone of the letter is not as formal as some other types of letters. Friendly letters can be written to someone you already know, or they can be written to someone you want to know better.

It is important to remember the five parts of the friendly letter. These are the *heading*, the *salutation*, the *body*, the *closing*, and the *signature*. Each section of the friendly letter has a purpose and is written in a specific place and order on the stationery.

Why all the fuss about how the letter is organized? It makes good sense; that's why. If you want to know who wrote a letter to you, it's important to know where to look for the signature—or maybe you already know who wrote the letter, but you want to know the person's address so you can write him or her back. If you know the five parts of the friendly letter and where to look for each one, it's easy to find whatever information you are looking for in the letter. Here is a closer look at those five parts:

☞ The **heading** is usually three lines. The first two lines are the address of the person who is writing the letter. The third line is the date the letter is written. A fourth line may be needed if the person writing is someone who lives in a foreign country. In this case, the date would be written on the fourth line of the heading.

☞ The **salutation**, or greeting, is the "Dear _____ " part of your letter. It's the section where you begin to say hello. A comma always follows the salutation of the friendly letter.

☞ The **body** is the main section of the letter. The body can be one paragraph or several paragraphs. This is where the author of the letter writes information for the person who is receiving the letter.

☞ The **closing** is where the writer begins to end the letter. The closing can be one word or several words, but only the first word of the closing is capitalized. A comma always follows the closing.

☞ The **signature** is the final section of the friendly letter. The signature lines up vertically with the heading and the closing of the letter. The writer signs his or her name after the closing. Except for mail that is sent electronically, the signature should be hand written. One easy way to learn the parts of the friendly letter is to memorize this sentence:

> **He saw beautiful cows singing.**

The first letter of each word represents a part of the friendly letter. For example, the letter **H** in the word "He" stands for the word "heading," the letter **s** in the word "saw" stands for "salutation," and so forth.

Now try creating a *mnemonic*, or memory, device of your own. On the lines below, write three sentences that will help you memorize the parts of the friendly letter.

1. _____

_____

2. _____

_____

3. _____

_____

The Parts of the Friendly Letter *(cont.)*

The following example illustrates all the parts of the friendly letter:

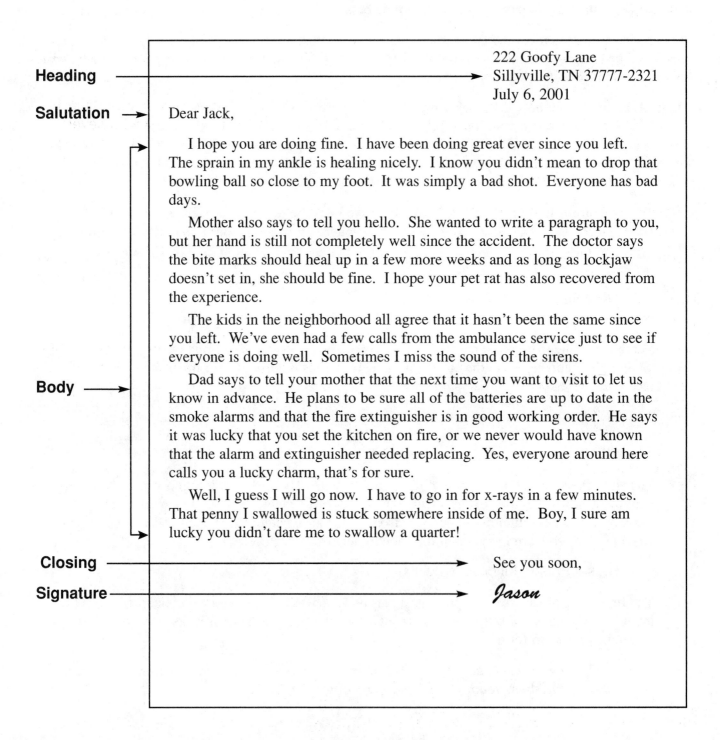

Heading

222 Goofy Lane
Sillyville, TN 37777-2321
July 6, 2001

Salutation

Dear Jack,

Body

I hope you are doing fine. I have been doing great ever since you left. The sprain in my ankle is healing nicely. I know you didn't mean to drop that bowling ball so close to my foot. It was simply a bad shot. Everyone has bad days.

Mother also says to tell you hello. She wanted to write a paragraph to you, but her hand is still not completely well since the accident. The doctor says the bite marks should heal up in a few more weeks and as long as lockjaw doesn't set in, she should be fine. I hope your pet rat has also recovered from the experience.

The kids in the neighborhood all agree that it hasn't been the same since you left. We've even had a few calls from the ambulance service just to see if everyone is doing well. Sometimes I miss the sound of the sirens.

Dad says to tell your mother that the next time you want to visit to let us know in advance. He plans to be sure all of the batteries are up to date in the smoke alarms and that the fire extinguisher is in good working order. He says it was lucky that you set the kitchen on fire, or we never would have known that the alarm and extinguisher needed replacing. Yes, everyone around here calls you a lucky charm, that's for sure.

Well, I guess I will go now. I have to go in for x-rays in a few minutes. That penny I swallowed is stuck somewhere inside of me. Boy, I sure am lucky you didn't dare me to swallow a quarter!

Closing

See you soon,

Signature

Jason

Notice the paragraphs are indented. This letter style is called semi-block style. When writing in semi-block style, indent to show when a new paragraph begins. Do not skip lines between paragraphs.

Writing a Friendly Letter That's Out of This World

Directions: Read the following story. Then follow the directions for Sections 1, 2, and 3 on page 8.

Your teacher has just written on the board that every student in the class will have a pen pal for the entire school year.

You groan! You moan! You had a pen pal in second grade when your teacher, Mrs. Munzo, made you write all year long to some girl named Greta who lived overseas but who never wrote you back even when you included a self-addressed stamped envelope with a picture of you and your little dog Ralphie tucked neatly inside. You don't need this type of hassle. You don't need or want another pen pal. You don't want this assignment.

You sigh. You roll your eyes. You look at your teacher. You really look at your teacher. Something is wrong with your teacher. Your teacher is not looking normal to you at all.

You rub your eyes. Are you seeing things? Where did she get that extra eyeball in the center of her head? Are those two antennas popping out from beneath her bouffant hair? And what happened to her skin? It was there just a second ago. Now she's covered in scales and slime, and she's slithering across the floor.

Before the entire class can pass out from shock, your teacher confesses to everyone that her other look had all been one really good costume and she is not who you thought she was. (Like you hadn't figured that one out already!) She goes on to tell you that the pen pals you will be writing aren't from this country. As a matter of fact, they aren't even from this planet. They're from a galaxy far, far away.

Still shocked and amazed by your teacher's new look, you are at least glad not to be working out of the book today. You begin to think this assignment might be pretty neat: a pen pal from another planet. Hmm . . . it's interesting. It has possibilities. Now, if only your teacher would stop slithering around the room, things might be okay.

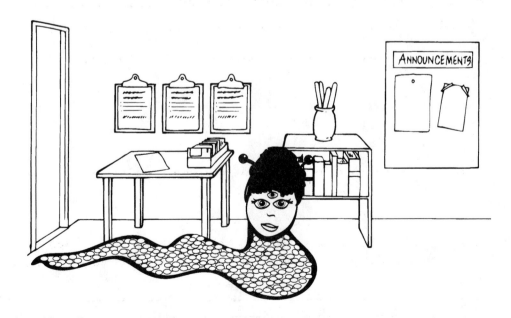

Writing a Friendly Letter
That's Out of This World *(cont.)*

Section 1

Stop and Think: If you could meet aliens from another planet, what questions would you ask them? What do you think they would look like? What would the aliens do in their spare time? On the lines provided, write five questions you would ask if you had the chance to correspond with an alien. Be sure to write your questions in complete sentences.

1. _____

_____

2. _____

_____

3. _____

_____

4. _____

_____

5. _____

_____

Section 2

Directions: On your own sheet of paper, write a friendly letter to your new pen pal from the planet Oxytania. Be sure to include the five parts of the friendly letter. Use at least two of your questions from Section 1 when writing the body of your letter. Include information about yourself and your own planet, as well.

Section 3

Just for Fun: In the frame below, draw a picture of your new pen pal.

Writing a Friendly Letter
That's Out of This World *(cont.)*

Sample Lesson Page

2345 Ed Harris Road
Clarksville, MO 87987-2143
June 8, 2004

Dear Marvin the Alien,

    I am so excited to have a pen pal from the planet Oxytania, but we were all a little shocked to discover our teacher was an alien. They've hired a substitute for her since she had to go back to your planet, but the substitute told us to continue with the lesson we had been assigned, so I still get to write you. Cool, huh?

    So what is it like in outer space? Do you have to go to school each day? Can you speak any languages besides your own? What do you do for fun?

    My friends and I hang out at the mall and play video games. We have to go to school. It's not as bad as it sounds because all of my friends are here.

    As long as you don't eat people, I would love to hear from you soon. I can't wait to learn as much as I can about you and your planet. If you do eat people, then just remember that I'm still pretty young and there's not a lot of meat yet on my bones. You might want to try my Aunt Martha's house instead.

Your new friend,

Freddy

A Closer Look

A good looking guy or girl, a hot pizza straight from the oven, a million dollars, or a huge plate of chocolate fudge—some things deserve a closer look. Such is the case with the five parts of a friendly letter. Knowing what to capitalize and where to put any punctuation is the key to helping you write a first-rate letter.

I. Heading

The first two lines of the heading are the address of the person who is writing the letter. The third line is the date. If you are writing to someone in a foreign country, the heading will include a fourth line. Remember these rules when writing the heading:

- The first word in each line is capitalized.

- There is no punctuation at the end of each line.

- A comma should be placed between the city and state, but not between the state and the zip code.

- A comma should be placed between the day of the month and the year.

Example: 888 Binkley Road

Thomasville, CO 54321-8764

February 25, 2002

Now it's your turn: On the lines below, write your address and today's date. Remember to punctuate correctly.

_____

_____

_____

II. Salutation

The salutation usually begins with the word "Dear," which is then followed by the name of the person to whom the letter is being written. Other things to remember when writing the salutation include the following:

- The word "Dear" and the recipient's name should always be capitalized.

- A comma follows the salutation of a friendly letter.

Examples: Dear Jacqueline,

Dear Ms. Garcia,

Now it's your turn: Pretend you are writing a letter to a person named Rufus. Write the salutation to your friendly letter here:

_____

A Closer Look *(cont.)*

III. Body

The body is the main part of the friendly letter; it is where the main information is contained.

- Each sentence should start with a capital letter.
- Paragraphs should be indented.
- Do not skip a line between paragraphs.

Now it's your turn: Pretend you have gone to the dentist and had a terrible visit. On the lines below, write at least two paragraphs to your friend Rufus telling him about your experience at the dentist's office. Remember, only write the body of the letter. (Use the back of this page, if necessary.)

_____

_____

_____

_____

_____

IV. Closing

The closing of the letter signals that the writer is almost finished.

- The first word should always be capitalized. Any subsequent words are written in lowercase letters.
- Put a comma at the end of the closing.
- Vertically align the closing with the heading.

  Examples: Sincerely,

  All my love,

  Yours truly,

Now it's your turn: Write a closing for a friendly letter here: _____

V. Signature

The signature is the final part of the friendly letter. It comes immediately after the closing. Do not skip a line between the closing and the signature. It should be in your own handwriting (unless the letter is an e-mail), and it should be aligned vertically with the heading and closing of the letter.

  Example: Your best friend,

  Stephanie

Now it's your turn: Write your signature here:_____

The Art of Writing Letters

Teacher Instruction Page

A letter is like a wrapped gift. What's inside is what counts, but the packaging is important, too.

How do you prove that to an audience of nonbelievers? Ask your principal to let you into the book room. Go and get a classroom set of English or literature books. Sift through the piles of books. Give half the class the dingiest books imaginable. You know the ones—they look like they've been used since World War II, and you wouldn't even rule out that possibility. Give the other half of the class the newest set of books. Watch half your class moan and complain while the other side brags and boasts. Be sure and tell the class you don't understand the problem. After all, the information inside is all the same.

Once you've shown them that in some instances appearances are important, tell them that today the class will be designing stationery for writing friendly letters.

❑ Have the class break into groups of three or four students.

❑ Pass out the worksheet entitled "The Art of Writing Letters."

❑ Give each group time to discuss ideas for designing the stationery.

❑ Each student in the group must make his/her own piece of stationery.

❑ No one is allowed to use the computer.

❑ Encourage the class to use craft items and natural resources. You may even want to take your class on a scavenger hunt around the school to search for items.

❑ Remind them that neatness is important.

Once the stationery is designed, have each student write a friendly letter on the paper. You may even be able to work with your school's art teacher and have students learn calligraphy during your unit on letter writing.

☞ **Extra Idea:** When students are finished with their letters you may want them to seal their letters in envelopes using wax and a special crest or insignia. Bring a candle to school. After you've received permission from your principal, a teacher or another adult should drip hot wax on the back flap of each of the envelopes. Students should not be allowed near the candle during this part of the activity. The teacher or another adult must be in charge of placing the hot wax on the envelopes. (Many art stores do furnish kits for this type of activity, but with careful preparation, a candle will work.)

Warn students that the wax is still hot. Again, with adult supervision, allow students to choose a design and let an adult place the crest into the wax to form a seal.

Students will be proud of the work they've done and will be extra careful before putting words on the stationery they've designed. Best of all, everyone will have learned the fine art of writing a letter.

The Art of Writing Letters *(cont.)*

Directions: Read the following questions. Discuss the questions with your group. Answer each question on the lines provided.

1. Why is it important for a letter to be written neatly?_____

_____

_____

2. Do you think a handwritten letter can look as nice as a typed letter? Why or why not?

_____

_____

_____

3. Which is more personal—a typed letter or a handwritten letter? Why? _____

_____

_____

4. If you were given a blank piece of paper and asked to create your own stationery, what pictures or designs would you include on the paper? _____

_____

_____

5. In the space below, draw or sketch a rough draft of your designs.

Friendly Doesn't Always Mean Nice

Some days even your best friend can get on your nerves.

Maybe it's one of those days where you woke up on the wrong side of the bed or the dog really did eat your homework or maybe your little brother lost his breakfast right in the middle of your backpack. Whatever the reason, whatever the cause, some days are just bad days; and even the people you like best better stay out of your way.

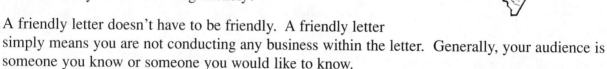

So what happens if you write a letter on a day when you aren't exactly being Prince Charming? Is it still a friendly letter even if you aren't feeling friendly?

A friendly letter doesn't have to be friendly. A friendly letter simply means you are not conducting any business within the letter. Generally, your audience is someone you know or someone you would like to know.

Regardless of the tone of your writing, you must still include all five parts of the friendly letter. Don't forget the five parts—in order—are the heading, the salutation, the body, the closing, and the signature. One good way to learn the five parts of the friendly letter is to practice them. Practice makes perfect, so even when you are writing a note to a friend who is sitting across the aisle from you (not that you would ever write notes in class) be sure and include all five parts of the letter. Don't forget to include commas after the salutation and the closing of your letter.

Directions: What type of things make you feel a little less than friendly? You know, those things that annoy you—like a bad hair day or having to babysit your baby brother on a Friday night.

In the space provided, list five things that really annoy you:

1. _____
2. _____
3. _____
4. _____
5. _____

Okay, now you are in "the mood." Imagine you are having the worst day ever. Maybe you sat in gum that was chewed by a person with definite salivation problems, or maybe during school you realized your shirt was on backwards. Whatever the reason, whoever is to blame, you are having a really bad day.

On a separate sheet of paper, write a friendly letter to someone you know. Tell that person all about your bad day. Be sure to include all five parts of the friendly letter.

Friendly Doesn't Always Mean Nice *(cont.)*

Sample Lesson Page

A Message from Melissa

P.O. Box 23
Coopertown, KY 34509-7676
August 18, 2003

Dear Carole,

You made me so angry today. I couldn't believe you laughed when I sat in gum. I've had to walk around all day with pink gum stuck to my white pants. Every time I tried to get up someone had to pull me out of the chair because my pants were so sticky. After the gum incident I figured what else bad could happen. Boy, was that a mistake.

As soon as I left gym class, I realized I had put my shirt on backwards, but the bell was about to ring so I didn't have time to change it. Then I went to language arts class, and I didn't have my homework. At the end of the day I was running for the bus, and I tripped and sprained my ankle. I yelled at you to wait for me, but I guess you didn't hear me.

It has been the worst day, and I'm still pretty upset with you. Write me back if you want. I only wrote you because I wanted you to know how upset I am.

Bye,

Melissa

Writing a Thank You Note . . .
Even If the Gift Was Strange

A thank you note is written in the same style as a friendly letter, which means it includes the five parts of the friendly letter: the heading, the salutation, the body, the closing, and the signature.

The purpose of the thank you note is to express thanks or appreciation. It should be written soon after receiving the gift or good deed. Thank you notes are generally handwritten and are usually on cards or stationery. The person writing the letter should always mention the gift or the deed in the note. Here is an example of a thank you note:

---

321 Powder Mill Lane
Pleasant City, MI 38901-9009
March 3, 2002

Dear Karen,

    Thank you so much for the wonderful gift you gave me for graduation. A photo album was such a great idea. I plan to put pictures of all of my family and friends in the album so that when I am away at school I can still see familiar faces.

    When I get back from my vacation we will have to get together and have lunch. I am sure I will have some pictures of the trip to share with you, and we can put them in my album together.

Thanks for everything,

Natalie

Learning to write a thank you note shows the world you have great manners, and writing a thank you note is easy when someone has given you a gift that truly was just what you always wanted. There are times, however, when a person has good intentions, but his or her gift may not be exactly what you had in mind. A thank you note is still appropriate if the person giving the gift was sincere. These are the hardest types of thank you notes to write, but they are just as important.

Directions: Read the story below and follow the directions for the activity that follows.

Your Aunt Janice knows that you've always loved milk. Going to the mailbox one day, you find a package, and by the return address you know that it's from Aunt Janice. You rip into the package, knowing it's going to be something fantastic!

What do you find? Under the layers of tissue paper there is a cowbell, a framed picture of a cow, and a card from Aunt Janice. Aunt Janice writes that she's coming to visit next week and when she does, she's bringing the dairy cow in the picture to you! The cow's name is Bessie, and she knows you'll love her just as much as you love milk. Aunt Janice thinks it will be a great experience for you to get your milk straight from the cow. Sure, it'll be a little more work, but think of all the other free foods you'll be able to make like ice cream, cheese, butter, and cream. If it's a dairy product, it can be yours.

What else can you do but put the cowbell in your room beside your new picture of Bessie and then go and clean out your refrigerator and freezer. Once Bessie arrives, it looks like you're going to need all the extra space in there that you can find.

Now if you only had a barn.

On a separate sheet of paper write a thank you note to Aunt Janice. Include all five parts of the thank you note. Make certain you are sincere in your note. After all, Aunt Janice was trying to be nice.

Writing a Thank You Note . . .
Even if the Gift Was Strange *(cont.)*

Sample Lesson Page

Scott's Scribbles

P.O. Box 398
Cumberland Road, TX 87693-0965
February 24, 2002

Dear Aunt Janice,

I was so surprised by the gift you sent me. It made me feel good to know that you think so much of me. The cowbell looks great on my dresser. I have it sitting beside the framed picture of Bessie. I'm sure Bessie is going to be a really nice cow. She has such friendly looking eyes. I even drew a sketch of her below. (Drawing class is really starting to pay off.)

Thank you again for thinking of me. I promise to take great care of Bessie. You take good care of yourself, and I promise to invite you over for that first glass of fresh milk.

Thanks again,

Scott

Minding Your Manners

If someone gave you a million dollars, you'd probably thank them, wouldn't you? Okay, you'd probably faint first, but then you would get up off the floor and thank them. The point is, you would definitely show some type of gratitude.

Good manners require you to say thank you whenever you receive a gift. Many people feel a verbal thank you is enough, but it is always appropriate to follow up with a written thank you note.

Not only do material gifts require a person to say thank you, but so do acts of kindness. Acts of kindness are those special things people do for you that cannot be bought in a store. A few examples are taking care of your pets while you're away on vacation, explaining a hard homework assignment, or washing the dishes for you even though it was really your turn. These everyday acts of kindness are oftentimes overlooked.

Directions: Read the following list. Think about each statement and then fill in the blanks. Next, complete the assignment that follows the list.

1. Someone at my house that I would like to do something nice for would be _____ because he/she is always _____.

2. Someone who is always doing kind things for me is _____.

3. The nicest compliment I ever received was from _____.

   He/she said _____.

4. If I did volunteer work, I would want to _____.

5. Someone at school I would like to do something nice for would be

   _____because_____.

6. Something good I could do for my community would be

   _____.

7. If I had to pick three things I wanted for my birthday, and none of the items could be things that could be purchased at a store, I would ask for

   _____, _____, and _____.

8. I think school would be a better place if everyone _____.

9. If I had to define the word "gift," I would say it is _____.

10. A famous person that always seems kind is _____

    because he/she_____.

To become more aware of the acts of kindness that occur in your life, keep a journal for one week. Write down the name of the person who is kind to you and what was done. Also keep a list of things you do for someone else. Hopefully, you will be surprised by how many good deeds you perform. When you're finished keeping your list, be sure and write at least one thank you note to someone who has been especially kind to you.

The Bread and Butter Note: It's Not for Breakfast

The bread and butter note sounds like something you might eat for breakfast with a heaping spoonful of jelly, but it's not. The bread and butter note is sent to the home of a friend or relative with whom you have recently visited. It is written to thank someone for his or her hospitality. It is different from a thank you note because the writer has usually not received a gift or material item. The bread and butter note is sent to thank family and friends for their kindness while you were their guest.

3636 Baptist Church Road
Center Point, NH 43590-6512
April 26, 2002

Dear Aunt Tessa,

    I had the best time ever at your beach house. Thank you for letting me stay with you for the week. I am so glad you knew what to do when that crab bit me on the toe. If you hadn't pried him off my foot, I would probably still be walking around with it hanging there.

    When I got home, Mom was surprised about my new pet rat, but she only stayed upset for a few days. I told her you had one, too. I don't know if that helped or not, but hopefully I will still get to come back again next year.

    Please tell everyone I said hello, and thank you again.

                      Love,

                      Sadie

Directions: Imagine you are back home after spending a week at your Uncle Elmo's emu ranch. In the space below, write a letter to your Uncle Elmo thanking him for his kindness and for letting you come and visit him at the ranch. Be sure and mention some of the adventures you had during your stay.

_____

_____

_____

_____

_____

_____

_____

_____

The Bread and Butter Note: It's Not for Breakfast *(cont.)*

Sample Lesson Page

1818 Bowling Avenue
Canton, OH 56389-8641
September 19, 2002

Dear Uncle Elmo,

Thank you for letting me visit you and Aunt Thelma Lou. I had a wonderful time. I can hardly wait until next year when it is time for me to visit again.

The emu farm is amazing. I had no idea that the emu so closely resembles the ostrich. Do you remember how I ran away when the one emu started chasing me? I still have the holes in my pants from where I tried to jump the fence for you to catch me, but the barbed wire caught me instead.

Thank you again for everything. I look forward to seeing you again. Be sure to write us soon and send pictures of Timmy. He is the best pet emu a boy could have. Too bad I couldn't bring him home with me, but I know an apartment is no place for him. I will talk to you soon.

Take care,

Mark

I Don't Know What to Say

There are times when you may have to write a friendly letter even when you don't have a lot to say. Maybe your mother thinks it's way past time you talked to your cousin Lou, or maybe your pen pal from Alaska has sent nearly triple the letters that you've written. Whatever the reason, it's always good to keep a list of topics handy so when you have to write a letter, you have something to write about.

Directions: Read the following topics. Write your answers on the lines provided.

1. Three things I enjoy doing in my spare time are _____,
_____, and _____.

2. My favorite movie, television show, and musical group are _____,
_____, and _____.

3. The scariest thing that ever happened to me was _____.

4. My favorite sports are _____ and _____.

5. If I could have any pet I want, I would get a _____
because _____.

6. If I had to describe my school in three words, I would say it is _____,
_____, and _____.

7. When I am older, I hope to live in _____
because _____.

8. The best book I ever read was _____.
I liked it because _____.

9. For fun, my friends and I like to _____.

10. The best surprise I ever had was when _____.

11. If I could pick my own name I would call myself _____.

12. Three things I think are really cool are _____,
_____, and _____.

13. Some of the places I have traveled to are _____.

14. My favorite subject in school is _____ because _____
_____.

15. If I could be like one other person, I would want to be like _____.

Use this information the next time you have to write a letter but don't know what to say. Share your answers with the person you are writing or ask them some of these same questions. Whether they answer seriously or humorously is not important. What matters is that you have something to say!

Getting Down to Business: Writing the Business Letter

A giant dinosaur ate your house. You decide to rearrange the furniture in your room and discover there really is a monster under the bed. You walk into class five minutes late, and the teacher says it's time for a quiz over what the class has just discussed.

Some things in life are serious.

Because life can be serious, there are times when you need to know how to do some serious writing. Thank goodness for the business letter. It can handle even the most serious situation.

The business letter is used for writing more formal correspondence. Most business letters are written in block style. This means that all parts of the letter, including the beginning of each paragraph, are lined up with the left margin.

The business letter has six parts. These parts are as follows:

I. the heading	IV. the body
II. the inside address	V. the closing
III. the salutation	VI. the signature

If you are writing a business letter, your audience is generally someone you do not know and you may or may not ever meet. The tone of the letter is usually serious and straightforward. Most people who are in business do not have a lot of extra time, so it is important to get straight to the point when writing a business letter. It is better to type the letter, but if it must be handwritten, use blue or black ink only.

Getting Down to Business: Writing the Business Letter *(cont.)*

The Six Parts of the Business Letter

I. Heading

The heading usually contains three lines. The first lines are the address of the person who is writing the letter. The last line is the date the letter is written.

II. Inside Address

The inside address is written below the heading. The inside address includes the name of the person to whom the letter is being written (if you know it), the name of the business, and the address of the business. The inside address is usually three or four lines.

III. Salutation

The salutation is the third part of the business letter. The salutation, or greeting of the business letter, is followed by a colon rather than a comma. It is written on the left-hand side of the paper and below the inside address. If you know the name of the person you are writing, be sure to use his or her name in the salutation. If you are unsure who will be receiving your letter, it is acceptable to put "Dear Sir or Madam" in place of the name.

IV. Body

The body follows the salutation of the business letter. Most business letters do not indent for paragraphs. Paragraphs are lined up with the left-hand margin of the paper. Double spacing is used between paragraphs to show the writer has begun a new thought. The writing in the body of the business letter should be clear and concise. Identify your purpose for writing the letter and do not waste time or space by including a lot of unnecessary information.

V. Closing

The closing of the letter may be one word or several words. Only the first word of the closing is capitalized. A comma always follows the closing. In a business letter the closing should be formal. Words such as "Sincerely" or "Cordially" are considered appropriate closings for a business letter. Cute phrases such as "Love ya" or "Catch you later" are not appropriate.

VI. Signature

The signature follows the closing of the business letter. The writer should skip four lines and then type or print his or her name. The signature lines up vertically with the closing. The letter should be signed in the space between the closing and the typed or printed name.

The author of a letter may feel he needs to include a phone number, e-mail address, etc. This information can be included in the heading of the letter. If this occurs, the heading becomes four lines in length instead of three lines. There may also be four lines if the writer is from a foreign country and needs to include this information in the heading.

Letters written on business stationery are written in the block style. When the information in the heading is already included on the stationery, all that needs to be added is the date. The rest of the letter will also follow the block format.

Getting Down to Business: Writing the Business Letter *(cont.)*

The following is an example of a business letter written in block style. Notice the paragraphs are not indented. A line is skipped when a new paragraph begins.

Heading →

Inside Address →

Salutation →

Body →

Closing →

Signature →

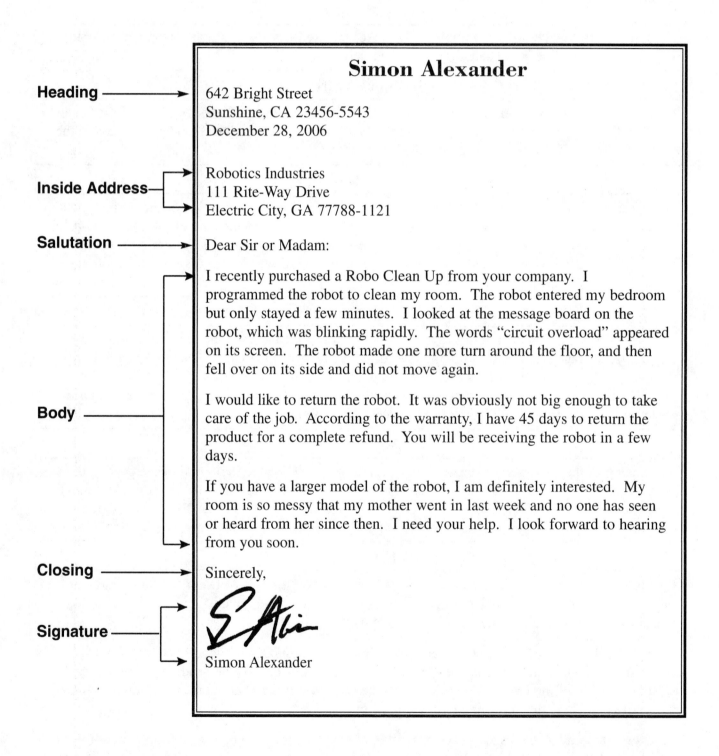

Simon Alexander

642 Bright Street
Sunshine, CA 23456-5543
December 28, 2006

Robotics Industries
111 Rite-Way Drive
Electric City, GA 77788-1121

Dear Sir or Madam:

I recently purchased a Robo Clean Up from your company. I programmed the robot to clean my room. The robot entered my bedroom but only stayed a few minutes. I looked at the message board on the robot, which was blinking rapidly. The words "circuit overload" appeared on its screen. The robot made one more turn around the floor, and then fell over on its side and did not move again.

I would like to return the robot. It was obviously not big enough to take care of the job. According to the warranty, I have 45 days to return the product for a complete refund. You will be receiving the robot in a few days.

If you have a larger model of the robot, I am definitely interested. My room is so messy that my mother went in last week and no one has seen or heard from her since then. I need your help. I look forward to hearing from you soon.

Sincerely,

Simon Alexander

Getting Down to Business: Writing the Business Letter *(cont.)*

Camp Fun-for-All is accepting applications. Every student that wants to attend the camp must write a business letter to the head director, Mrs. Fisher. The camp is located at 22 Blossom Lane in Nashville, Tennessee 34444-5412.

Everyone wants to go to Camp Fun-for-All. There's no other camp where you get to practice yodeling for two hours each day, knit socks for all of your holiday gift giving, and practice building fires without any matches while standing under a waterfall. Every camper who successfully completes the rigorous activities at Camp Fun-for-All is automatically invited back next year. What could be more fun?

Directions: In the blanks provided, write a business letter to the director of Camp Fun-for-All. Convince her that you should be allowed to attend the summer camp. Some of the letter has already been completed for you.

_____

_____

_____

Mrs. Fisher, Camp Director

_____

22 Blossom Lane

_____

Dear _____ :

_____

_____

_____

_____

_____

Sincerely,

_____

_____

_____

Getting Down to Business: Writing the Business Letter *(cont.)*

Sample Lesson Page

---

78 Twin Oaks Drive

Lexington, MA 79034-1111

July 16, 2003

Mrs. Fisher, Camp Director

Camp Fun-for-All

22 Blossom Lane

Nashville, TN 34444-5476

Dear Mrs. Fisher:

I want to attend Camp Fun-for-All this summer. Please send me an application for your camp. Several of my friends have attended Camp Fun-for-All, and I've only heard positive things about their camping experiences.

Last year, I was the yodeling champion for my county, but I know I could use the extra practice I would get at Camp Fun-for-All. I also enjoy knitting, and I can't wait to make my holiday gifts while staying at your camp.

Please send me my application as soon as you can. I look forward to hearing from you soon. I anxiously await your response.

Sincerely,

Robert Taylor

Robert Taylor

Letters Have Style

Magazines tell you what's hot and what's not. Television shows you all the latest trends. Style is everywhere you look. So it's not surprising to find that even letters have style.

Although there are several styles for writing letters, there are two that are most often used. These are the block style for business letters and the semi-block style for friendly letters.

Directions: On the sample layouts below, label the 6 parts of the business letter and the 5 parts of the friendly letter.

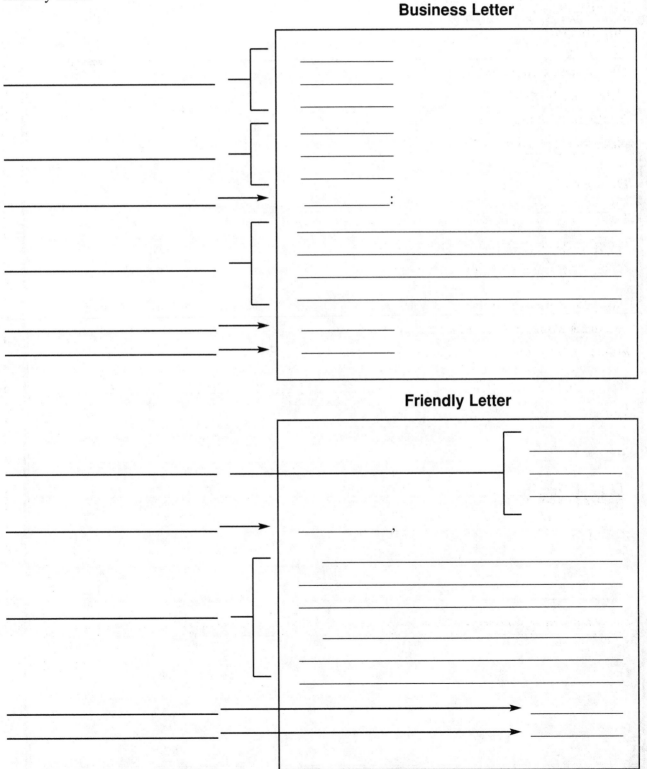

Business Letter

Friendly Letter

Letters Have Style *(cont.)*

Directions: Read over the information given and then complete the block style business letter.

On May 12, 2004, Sandy Campbell—who lives at 456 Hampton Circle in Clairmont, Washington, 76768-6732—wrote to Chocolate King, a company that makes over fifty-two different types of chocolate candy bars. The company's address is 111 Heavenly Place, Fudge Town, Ohio 90876-1212.

Ms. Campbell wrote to complain about how much weight she had put on since she began eating Chocolate King's candy bars. She claimed the chocolate is addictive, and she felt the company should pay for her new weight loss program.

_____

_____

_____

_____

_____

_____

_____ :

_____

_____

_____

_____

_____

_____

_____

_____ ,

_____

Letters Have Style *(cont.)*

Sample Lesson Page

From the Desk of Sandy Campbell

456 Hampton Circle
Clairmont, WA 76768-6732
May 12, 2004

Chocolate King
111 Heavenly Place
Fudge Town, OH 90876-1212

Dear Sir or Madam:

I am writing to complain about your candy bars. Although the candy bars are delicious, I believe each bar should contain a warning label. The chocolate is so delicious that it is addictive. Because of Chocolate King's candy bars, I have gained over fifty pounds!

I have joined a weight loss program because of the extra weight I have gained. The program is expensive, and I believe Chocolate King should reimburse me for the cost. It is the responsibility of the manufacturer to warn unsuspecting buyers about the hazards of its products. Excessive weight gain can lead to all types of medical problems. I would not be facing these risks if it weren't for your candy bars.

Sincerely,

Sandy Campbell

Sandy Campbell

Soap Suds in My Mouth: Writing a Letter of Complaint

When you feel someone has done you an injustice or a disservice, you have the right to complain—but you need to do so in the proper manner. A letter of complaint is one way to handle a situation that you feel has not gone the way it should. Letters of complaint are written in the same style as the business letter. This means they should contain all six parts of the business letter: the heading, the inside address, the salutation, the body, the closing, and the signature.

A well-written complaint gives clear reasons for a person's concerns. The letter should explain what happened and why there is a problem. The writer might offer a solution to the problem, and no matter how angry or upset the person is, he should thank the reader for his or her time.

Although a letter of complaint is usually negative, it never hurts to remember the old saying, you catch more flies with honey. If you try to maintain a degree of sincerity in your letter, your complaint will be taken more seriously. The following is an example of a letter of complaint:

---

111 Itchy Avenue
Scratch City, AL 23233-7254
February 3, 2007

Fido Soap Company
Dogwood Lane
Canine, CA 57894-4809

Dear Sir or Madam:

I wish to complain about a recent incident I had involving one of your products. Fido Soap Company has long been known for its dog shampoos that are guaranteed to help keep any pooch looking shiny and clean. Dogs that use Fido Soap look clean enough to eat off of—or so I thought.

After a night on the town, some friends and I decided to dine out on a little Chihuahua dog named Tiny. We had seen her owner give her a bath a few hours before, and we'd read the label on the bottle of shampoo. It was Fido Soap, so we knew the dog's coat would be in great condition. Little did we realize Fido Soap had recently added a new scent to their usual soap. We took one bite; and instead of the delicious dinner we expected, all we got was a mouth full of soapsuds and fresh flower scent. Let me tell you, it was disgusting!

As a flea, I frequently dine on dogs that use your products, and I must tell you that the new flower scent is a big disappointment. The new shampoo apparently does not rinse out well either, because I dined that night on three dogs that had all been bathed with Fido Soap; each and every one left a soapy taste in my mouth.

Go back to using the old stuff. It made the dogs look pretty, and it made me smile.

Thank you for your time. I look forward to hearing from you soon.

Sincerely,

Flea Bite

Flea Bite

Soap Suds in My Mouth:
Writing a Letter of Complaint *(cont.)*

Part 1

Directions: On the lines provided, list 10 situations where someone might need to write a letter of complaint.

Example: You went to the movies for a nice evening out, but the theater was filthy.

Reasons to Write a Letter of Complaint

1. _____

2. _____

3. _____

4. _____

5. _____

6. _____

7. _____

8. _____

9. _____

10. _____

Part 2

Directions: Choose one of the reasons from Part 1, and on your own sheet of paper, write a letter of complaint.

Soap Suds in My Mouth:
Writing a Letter of Complaint *(cont.)*

Sample Lesson Page

P.O. Box 98
Silverton, SC 74561-8988
October 9, 2003

Brenda's House of Beauty
657 Haywood Lane
Silverton, SC 74561-8988

Dear Madam:

I recently visited your hair salon to have curl added to my hair. Marcia, the stylist who did my hair, apparently did something wrong. Instead of having more curl, I now have hair that is straight as a stick. I am not happy about this.

The minute I arrived home, the curl started falling out of my hair. By that evening my hair was straight. I tried to call Marcia and talk to her about refunding my money, but she was rude and not at all helpful. Since she does not own the salon, I decided to turn to you for help.

I have always received good service at Brenda's, but I am disappointed with my new look. I would like a full refund of my money. I do not believe I should have to pay for something that I did not get.

Sincerely,

Barbara Kelly

Barbara Kelly

Writing a Business Letter That Gets Noticed

You were hungry. You had a craving for a home-cooked meal. So what could you do? You decided to try out that restaurant everyone's been raving about—the one that advertises meals like your grandmother makes: Ma and Pa's Kettle.

The minute you walked through the door, you could smell something good. You ordered a big glass of tea, mashed potatoes and gravy, biscuits, and fried chicken. It was looking good, too, when they put the food in front of your face. You dove in without hesitation. Your spoon was loaded with a great big serving of mashed potatoes. It did taste like Granny's cooking. It tasted just like Granny's cooking! The problem is, your granny can't cook. You were hoping the food would taste like someone else's grandmother's cooking!

There were lumps in the potatoes, and the gravy was cold. The chicken was so greasy that it kept sliding out of your fingers and back onto your plate.

You left the restaurant sick, upset, and still hungry. What could you do? Where could you turn for help?

Then an idea came to you. You remembered sitting in English class, listening to your teacher rattle on and on that some day you would need to know how to write a business letter. Some day you might need to get a job or make a complaint! (Gee, whoever thought you'd really use some of that stuff they teach in school?)

Directions: Write a business letter to Ma and Pa's Kettle complaining about your dining experience. Remember to follow all the rules of the business letter. Don't forget to include the six sections of the business letter: the heading, the inside address, the salutation, the body, the closing, and the signature. You may use the back of this sheet or write your letter on a separate piece of paper.

Writing a Business Letter That Gets Noticed *(cont.)*

Sample Lesson Page

◆ ◆ ◆ ◆ ◆ Greetings from Gail! ◆ ◆ ◆ ◆ ◆

63 Kensington Avenue
Jackson, WA 60321-2341
July 16, 2005

Ma and Pa's Kettle
167 Main Street
Bakersville, WA 60321-3455

Dear Ma and Pa:

I recently dined at your restaurant, and I had an interesting experience. I had heard only good things about your establishment, so I decided to try it out for myself. Little did I know my meal would turn out to be so bad.

I ordered the hungry man's special. The special included a large helping of mashed potatoes. I dove in with my fork and after only one large bite of the potatoes, I found huge lumps in my food. The gravy was cold, and the chicken was greasy. The only edible item on my plate was the sprig of parsley.

Your restaurant has a good reputation, and I wish only good things for you in the future, but I did want you to know about my dining experience. I left your restaurant feeling hungry and upset. That's not the way I thought a customer should feel after dining at Ma and Pa's Kettle.

Sincerely,

Gail James

Gail James

To, From, and Regarding: The Business Memo

Some days there just isn't enough time to do everything that needs to be done. The idea of writing a lengthy business letter can seem like an overwhelming task even if you have something that really needs to be said. It's times like these when the business memo comes in handy.

The memo is quicker to write than the business letter. It is usually no longer than one page in length. The beginning of the memo states the name of the person(s) who will receive the letter, who the letter is from, and what the letter is regarding. The sender will sign or initial by his name rather than signing at the bottom of the memo. There is no rule for when to send a business memo instead of a business letter, although memos are considered to be more informal. It is important to note that the memo does not allow for the sender's address to be placed on the actual letter. If the writer is worried that the envelope may become separated from the letter, it is best to send a formal letter with a return address.

May 15, 2004

To: Blood Donor Services

From: Ima Mosquito

Re: Blood Identification Problem

I heard through the grapevine that your company, Blood Donor Services, was having some problems with the lab equipment you use to identify particular blood types. Knowing what type of blood you draw from a volunteer is, of course, vital to your business. After all, you can't give someone with A-positive blood, B-negative blood. The results could be fatal.

I would like to volunteer my services to your company. Since I am a mosquito, I am extremely mobile. I can get in and get out before a person even knows I'm there. You would have no more of that silly fainting business you have when someone sees one of those big, sharp needles coming at him. Except for a small itch later, the person would never even know I had been there.

After my withdrawal, I would be more than willing to inform you what blood type the candidate has.

I look forward to hearing from you.

To, From, and Regarding:
The Business Memo *(cont.)*

Directions: In the space below, write a memo to your teacher with a clever excuse for why you have not turned in your homework for the entire school week.

To: _____

From:_____

Re:_____

To, From, and Regarding:
The Business Memo *(cont.)*

Sample Lesson Page

To: Mr. Davidson

From: Claudia Cannon

Re: Missing Assignments

For the past few days, I have not turned in any of my homework assignments. I feel the zeroes I have received are somewhat unfair since no one ever asked me why my homework was not complete. I feel my reasons are good enough that I should be allowed an extension for the due date of my homework.

Last week, my brother received a pet snake for his eighth birthday. Boga, the snake, is approximately three feet long. Boga, apparently, did not like his cage; and after only one night, he escaped into the house. We searched everywhere for the snake, but we had no luck in locating him.

I went to bed with great reluctance, but exhaustion finally overtook me. Sometime during the night, I felt a tickling sensation around my toes. It did not take me long until the same sensation was at my nose. I tried to rub my nose, but it didn't help. I was still half asleep, but I managed to open my eyes and look. Imagine my surprise to see a snake resting beside me in my bed! Although I was frightened, I think I could have handled the snake being in my bed if it hadn't been for the other little surprise.

In the mouth of the snake was a half-eaten mouse. Its tail was hanging out of the mouth of the snake, and its tiny tail was what had tickled my face. It was simply too much. I ran from the room screaming at the top of my lungs.

My brother finally recovered his snake yesterday, and it is now safely tucked away in its new cage. However, during the ordeal, I refused to go back into my room until the snake was found. All of my schoolbooks were in the corner of my bedroom. I felt my homework was important, but I felt my life was even more important.

I hope this clears up any misunderstanding you may have had about my reasons for not doing my homework.

Short and Sweet:
Using Abbreviations and Notations

Since the day you began school, you've seen notes passed on the playground, on the bus, and yes, even in class. Some notes were short and sweet; others were long and complicated. Many contained two letters at the very end: P.S. The P.S. lets the reader know there is still more to come.

P.S. is an abbreviation for the Latin based word *postscript*. *Post* means "after" and *script* means "writing," so a P.S. is writing that is done after the rest of the letter. Over time, the word was shortened to the two letters seen on much of today's mail.

People that write letters use many other abbreviations or notations besides P.S. Below is a list of other commonly used abbreviations and their meanings:

SASE—self addressed, stamped envelope

SAE—self addressed envelope

P.O. Box—post office box

The following abbreviations are written after the signature of a business letter:

Enc.—enclosure

Att.—attached

CC—copies

The abbreviations *enc.* and *att.* let the reader know he or she should look for something in the envelope other than the letter. Before copy machines, carbon copies were used to make duplicates. This is why the abbreviation for copies is CC.

Some parts of the address may also be abbreviated. States are commonly abbreviated, but it is better to write out the name of the month, the name of the city, and the name of the street. If the two-letter abbreviation is used for the name of the state, no period is needed after the abbreviation.

Another abbreviation you may see after the signature is a set of initials. The initials represent the sender of the letter and the typist. The initials of the typist are typed in lower case letters (for example, SC/jkp).

Short and Sweet:
Using Abbreviations and Notations *(cont.)*

A Quick Reference for State Abbreviations

If you use the two-letter state abbreviation, be sure and write the abbreviation correctly. The two letters should be capitalized, and there are no periods or other punctuation between the letters or after the letters.

Incorrect: T.N.	*Incorrect*: TN.
Incorrect: Tn.	*Correct*: TN

Use the following chart whenever you need to find the two-letter abbreviation for one of the fifty states.

Alabama	AL		Nebraska	NE
Alaska	AK		Nevada	NV
Arizona	AZ		New Hampshire	NH
Arkansas	AR		New Jersey	NJ
California	CA		New Mexico	NM
Colorado	CO		New York	NY
Connecticut	CT		North Carolina	NC
Delaware	DE		North Dakota	ND
Florida	FL		Ohio	OH
Georgia	GA		Oklahoma	OK
Hawaii	HI		Oregon	OR
Idaho	ID		Pennsylvania	PA
Illinois	IL		Rhode Island	RI
Indiana	IN		South Carolina	SC
Iowa	IA		South Dakota	SD
Kansas	KS		Tennessee	TN
Kentucky	KY		Texas	TX
Louisiana	LA		Utah	UT
Maine	ME		Vermont	VT
Maryland	MD		Virginia	VA
Massachusetts	MA		Washington	WA
Michigan	MI		West Virginia	WV
Minnesota	MN		Wisconsin	WI
Mississippi	MS		Wyoming	WY
Missouri	MO		The District of Columbia	DC
Montana	MT			

Short and Sweet:
Using Abbreviations and Notations *(cont.)*

Directions: Read the following questions and fill in the blanks with the correct answers.

1. Notations in business letters are found after the _____ of the letter, which is the end of the letter.

2. TN, GA, KY, and UT are all examples of _____ abbreviations.

3. The abbreviation SASE stands for _____

_____.

4. If copies of a letter have been sent to other people, the abbreviation _____ will appear at the end of the letter.

5. The abbreviation *enc.* stands for the word_____.

6. If someone does not require postage on a return envelope they might use the abbreviation _____.

7. In letter writing, abbreviations that are written after the signature are called

_____.

8. It is better not to abbreviate the month, the _____and the _____.

9. Mail delivered to the post office rather than a street address is delivered to a _____ box.

10. If a check or money order was sent in a business letter, the abbreviation _____ should appear after the signature.

11. MN is the correct abbreviation for what state?_____.

12. What is the correct abbreviation for North Carolina?_____.

The Envelope:
It's for More Than Just Licking

The envelope: you lick it, you seal it, and you toss it in the mailbox. The envelope is all that stands between your letter and a hundred other peering eyes. It is an important part of the letter-writing process; and yet, sadly, it is often ignored. Don't believe it? Ask yourself, when was the last time you saw an envelope smile? They definitely feel ignored.

There are many different types of envelopes available for mailing letters. The envelope should be approximately the same width as the letter that is being mailed. It is important to know how to address the envelope if you want your mail to arrive at the correct location.

Each envelope should contain two addresses. The return address is written in the upper left-hand corner. This is the address of the person who is mailing the letter. The second address goes near the center of the envelope. This is the address of the person who is receiving the letter. Both addresses must be complete or the post office will return the mail to the sender.

Ramona Cross
765 Beach Boulevard
Mexico Beach, FL 87432-5554

Scott G. Moore
P.O. Box 567
Cairo, GA 56421-1212

☞ Include a first and last name in the return address.

☞ Do not put any punctuation at the end of each line.

☞ Do put a comma between the city and the state.

☞ Never put a comma between the state and the zip code.

☞ Do not write the mailing address too near the top of the envelope. The post office needs this space for the postage and their date stamp.

☞ If you write the address instead of typing it, write legibly. If the address cannot be read, the envelope cannot be delivered.

☞ The mailing address is usually three or four lines. If the letter is sent to a business, the first line may have the name of the person at the company that you wish to receive the letter. In that case, the second line should be the name of the business.

The Envelope:
It's for More Than Just Licking *(cont.)*

Part 1

Directions: Pretend you have to mail a letter to the principal at your school. Write the correct return address and mailing address on the envelope below.

Part 2

Directions: Fill in the envelope below with the correct information. Wendy Britt—who lives at 21 Davis Street, Nashville, Tennessee 35671-0276—is writing a letter to her best friend, Ann Crede. Ann lives at 700 Robin Lane, Carrington, Nevada 67439-1243.

Filling Out Forms

You can get five bazillion CDs or cassettes for only one penny if you simply fill out this form and mail it today!

Does this sound too good to be true?

It probably is; but there will be times when you will need to know how to fill out a form to get what you want.

People of all ages need to know how to fill out forms. Students are often asked to fill out forms or applications before they can join a club or belong to a sports team. Knowing how to accurately give information on an application is invaluable in situations like these.

When filling out an application or form, here are some helpful hints you need to remember:

- ❏ Unless pencil is requested, use blue or black ink.
- ❏ Fill in all lines accurately and completely.
- ❏ Use correct grammar and spelling.
- ❏ Do not give false information.
- ❏ Print. Do not write in cursive unless it is requested.

Directions: Read the following story, and then fill out the application on page 44.

Camp Freedom Wants You!

For years you've wanted to go away to summer camp. You've dreamed of it. You've planned for it. You've had your bag packed and under the bed ever since you first heard of it. Now, finally, after three summers of continuous begging, your parents have agreed. You are going to Camp Freedom.

What's so great about Camp Freedom? There's no bugle blowing at five in the morning. Campers can sleep until noon. There are no rules except to have fun. The food is delivered from the nearest pizza parlor, and desserts are always available in the mess hall. The barracks are condos that sit on the ocean, and each room comes equipped with a big screen television.

There's just one little problem: camp doesn't begin for an entire year!

Filling Out Forms *(cont.)*

Application for Camp Freedom

Name: _____

               Last   First   Middle

Date of Birth: _____ Male: _____ Female: _____

Address: _____

              Street/P.O. Box   Apt. #

_____

            City   State   Zip Code

Phone #: _____ Parent's Work Number: _____

Parent's/Guardian's Name: _____ Relationship: _____

Name of School: _____ Grade: _____

Hobbies or Interests: _____

Person to Contact in Case of an Emergency: _____

Relationship: _____ Phone #: _____

In your own words, explain why you want to attend Camp Freedom:

_____

_____

_____

_____

_____

_____

Signature of Applicant: _____

Signature of Parent/Guardian: _____

Filling Out Forms *(cont.)*

Directions: Read the information below, and then complete the form on page 46.

Join the Hare Club for Them

It's time for people to take a stand and support their local rabbits. Rabbits have rights, and it's about time people started listening. Rabbits are cute, funny, cuddly, and loveable. No longer should these animals be chased from gardens by farmers with weapons. No longer should these adorable creatures be served as any type of main menu item or used as clothing to warm someone else's body. Rabbits were not meant to be persecuted.

You can help rabbits earn the rights they deserve. Join the Hare Club for Them. It's the only club that shows you care for hares.

◆ Free carrots for all rabbits. (Rabbits look so cute when they're eating.)

◆ Reduced prices at ear piercing salons. (They do have a lot to pierce.)

◆ Cheap dry cleaning bills. (Rabbits get fur on everything they wear.)

◆ And, of course, free chocolate eggs when they're in season.

Filling Out Forms *(cont.)*

Hare Club Application

Name: _____
               Last   First   Middle

Date of Birth: _____ Male _____ Female: _____

Address: _____
              Street/P.O. Box   Apt. #

_____
          City   State   Zip Code

Phone #: _____ Parent's Work Number: _____

Parent's/Guardian's Name: _____ Relationship: _____

Name of School: _____ Grade: _____

Hobbies or Interests: _____

Person to Contact in Case of an Emergency: _____

Relationship: _____ Phone #: _____

Please print your answers to the following questions:

  1. Have you ever eaten rabbit? _____

  2. Who is your favorite rabbit in the entertainment industry? _____

  3. Have you or anyone in your family ever worked at a carrot factory? _____

At the Hare Club, our motto is "It's better to have hares than no hares at all." In your own handwriting, tell what this statement means to you.

_____

_____

_____

Signature of Applicant: _____

Signature of Parent/Guardian: _____

* Applications for the Hare Club will be processed on a first come, first serve basis. New members will be notified by mail.

The Importance of Tone And the Author's Purpose

> *Go to the office, now!*

> *Please, go to the office.*

> *Please, go to the office.*

These three sentences all mean the same thing, sort of. In all three sentences, someone needs to go to the office, but it is the tone of the three statements that is different. Tone in writing is how a person expresses his or her thoughts or ideas. It can show such emotions as love, hate, confusion, despair, happiness, sadness, and hopefulness. The tone also helps state the author's purpose in writing. It lets the reader know if he's writing to entertain, to amuse, to express anger, to inform, etc.

The first sentence—Go to the office, now!—is a command. You can imagine that the speaker is yelling. The tone is full of urgency. The second sentence is a request. This person is asking nicely, "Please, go to the office." The final sentence is a statement of fact. The writer is informing the person that he needs to go to the office. The person is neither yelling nor being extremely kind. He or she is stating what needs to be done.

The importance of tone when writing a letter simply cannot be overlooked. The tone of the writer's words sets the mood for the entire letter. Tone helps define the purpose of why a person is writing a letter. To write a letter of complaint, you need to use a more aggressive tone of writing; however, to write a letter asking for a job, you would need to use a friendlier, more professional tone.

Complete the worksheet on page 48. Determine the tone used by the authors of each paragraph. An example is provided.

The Importance of Tone
And the Author's Purpose *(cont.)*

Directions: Read the following sentences. On the lines provided, identify the tone that is being used in each paragraph. There may be several different answers.

Example: We had the best time ever. The swimming and the fishing were just wonderful. Uncle James was hilarious when he started barking like a dog. I know it taught me never to get hypnotized in front of a large crowd, that's for sure.

Answer: happy, silly, friendly

1. The service was horrible. I had to wait for over three hours before one of the technicians would take a look at my car. When I finally did get to talk to someone, I was told the shop was closing in fifteen minutes and that I would need to come back the next day.
   Answer:_____

2. I cried the minute we left. It was so hard to think that I might never see you again. I know you hate to fly, but you simply must come and see me as soon as you can, and I promise I will come and visit you soon.
   Answer:_____

3. There's always a silver lining. I know things look bad right now, but you just need to hang in there. Time heals all wounds. I know things will get better for you.
   Answer:_____

4. My references are all included. I have worked for several years in my current position, but I am looking for a change. I am a hard worker, and I don't mind starting at an entry-level position and working my way up in the company.
   Answer:_____

5. I adore you. You fill my every waking moment with thoughts of our love. No one has ever made me want to write poetry and sing songs of love the way you do.
   Answer:_____

6. You can't tell me what to do. I don't have to listen to you, and you can't make me. You can take your rules and get out of my face.
   Answer:_____

7. Every strand of hair in my head fell out! It was the worst experience of my life. I will never visit that hairstylist again, and I certainly would not recommend the establishment to any of my friends. I might, however, recommend it to a few of my enemies.
   Answer:_____

8. Dinner was simply delicious. It's so nice to spend an evening with friends. I can't remember the last time I had a more enjoyable time.
   Answer:_____

9. I laughed until I almost cried. I wish you could have seen Jack when he put the green peas up his nose. All of the people in the cafe were looking at us, especially when Jack laughed so hard that one of the peas shot out of his nose and straight into the hair of the unsuspecting waiter!
   Answer:_____

10. I know my face had to be red. I couldn't believe my zipper was undone and no one told me. From now on, I'm only wearing clothes with buttons.
    Answer:_____

Hire Me, I'm Nice: Writing a Resume

Unless you happen to know a friend or relative who is hiring, getting a job is not always easy. It takes more to get a job than simply being a nice person. Most companies will require you to show how qualified you are for the job you want. Most will want to know your educational background and other job-related experiences that you've had.

Employers do not expect students to have extensive work experience, but they do want a resume that shows you have experience as a leader and that you would be a benefit to the company if they hired you.

Not every job requires a resume. Many jobs only require that you fill out an application. However, it is a good idea to have an updated resume on file at all times so that when a job becomes available that does require a resume, you are ready to go. Remember these helpful hints when writing your own resume:

- ❑ A resume lists a person's qualifications for a job.

- ❑ It includes a person's name, address, and telephone number.

- ❑ It includes a person's educational information and previous work experience.

- ❑ Information on a resume should be listed in chronological order, listing the most recent experiences first.

On a resume, do not include your work experience if it is not relative to the job you are trying to get. As a person gains more education, it is no longer necessary to include information such as middle school attended, etc. However, if you are a student in high school and you are trying to get a job as a counselor at a summer camp, this type of information is relevant to your resume.

A resume should always be typed, and it should be no longer than one page. There is no one correct style for a resume, but information should be neatly arranged on the page. Remember that you are trying to persuade someone to hire you, so be sure and emphasize any qualifications you might have that will help you get the job. A student looking for a job may want to include on his or her resume items such as community service or future goals.

Some companies may ask for a written reference from your friends, family, or past employers. A written reference is a letter from someone that recommends you as a good employee or worker. Others may ask for a list of names and phone numbers of your references so that the employer can call and speak personally to the references you have given.

Hire Me, I'm Nice: Writing a Resume *(cont.)*

Teacher Instruction Page

Since many students do not yet work, one way to practice resume writing is to have students pick a career they might be interested in pursuing in the future. With the help of the class, list several possible career choices on the board or overhead. Next, pass out sections of the classifieds to the students. Explain how the classifieds are organized. Show students how to find jobs that have been listed on the board. Next, look for jobs that no one has mentioned.

After students have seen what types of jobs are available, you can assign careers in one of two ways:

1. Have students look through the classifieds and decide on a job.

2. Have students draw from a collection of classified advertisements that you have previously cut out and gathered.

When students decide on jobs, help them determine what type of education, work experience, etc., they will need for the job. Encourage students to be creative and make up whatever information they will need for their resume.

Have students create their own resumes by studying the sample resume on page 51. If students do not have access to a computer, you may want to allow the resumes to be handwritten.

For an optional activity, hand out only five or six different job descriptions to the entire class. This way several students will apply for the same job. Determine which students have the same jobs and set up a date for students to interview for the position. The teacher can act as the employer, or another adult can be invited to the classroom to help with this activity. Have the students interview for the jobs and compare their resumes to determine who gets "hired" for the position.

Hire Me, I'm Nice: Writing a Resume *(cont.)*

Sample Lesson Page

Irene Wilson

2102 Beach Avenue

Cedar Hill, MI 65412

(617) 555-4789

Education

Grady High School (1995–1999)

Activities

Beta Club, President (1998–1999)

Junior Classical League, Secretary (1997–1998)

Work Experience

Volunteer Worker (July, 1999)

   Served as a candy striper at the Cedar Hill Medical Center. Worked in the pediatric unit each day. Answered telephones and helped read to the children each afternoon.

Secretarial Work (July, 1998)

Worked for a home-based company. Helped do computer work and write bills to customers.

Summer School Tutor (August, 1997)

   Worked at Grady High School in the English department. Helped students in peer tutoring groups. Helped teacher with paper work and did some computer work.

References

References available upon request.

Faster Than the Pony Express: Sending E-Mail

If you own a computer, chances are you've either sent or received e-mail. What's so special about e-mail? It's fast and convenient. E-mail messages are received instantly; and depending on the computer used, you can also send and receive pictures and voice messages with your mail. Traditional snail mail simply can't compare to the speed of the computer.

Writing a letter that is to be sent by e-mail is a little different than writing a letter that is to be sent through the postal service. One of the main differences is that all e-mailed letters are typed. Another obvious difference is there is no stamp or envelope needed. There are a few rules you need to follow when sending and receiving e-mail.

❑ Do not write in all capital letters. IT LOOKS LIKE YOU ARE YELLING WHEN YOU DO THIS!

❑ Do include a salutation. It makes the letter more personal.

❑ Do use correct capitalization and punctuation.

❑ Do check your spelling.

❑ Do not say anything you might regret. Once you hit the send button, your e-mail has been electronically mailed.

❑ Do reply promptly to e-mail that requires a response from you.

E-mail does not require a written signature. Since the letter is not printed on paper, a signature is not required. You can, of course, type your name at the end of the letter if you wish. Also, you do not need to include the date. Mail that is sent via the computer automatically includes the date. If you are planning to send an e-mail, the screen will show a display that looks similar to this:

Send To:

Subject:

The e-mail address of the person who is receiving the letter should be placed in the "send to" box. You do not have to fill in the "subject" box, but it is a good idea to put some type of note to let the reader know what the letter will be about. For example, if you are writing to tell the person about your dog's trip to the veterinarian, you might write "Duncan's checkup."

Faster Than the Pony Express: Sending E-Mail *(cont.)*

Directions: Your best friend, Taylor, has just moved to Florida and can't wait to hear from you and catch up on all the gossip at school. Your parents won't let you make any long distance calls, and you're too cheap to go and buy a stamp. Thank goodness for e-mail.

Taylor's e-mail address is QTPie@abc.com. Write Taylor a letter on your computer screen below. Use your imagination and pretend it's a laptop computer.

Send to: [   ]

Subject: [   ]

[   ]

Faster Than the Pony Express: Sending E-Mail *(cont.)*

Sample Lesson Page

Send To: | QTPie@abc.com

Subject: | Problems at my house

Dear Taylor,

I hope you are doing well in Florida. Since you moved, things here haven't been the same. Everyone at school misses you, and they all wanted me to tell you they send their best wishes.

I hope I will get to see you this summer when we go on vacation, but I'm not sure if we are going to get to go on a vacation or not. My little brother, Bobby, has been grounded, and Dad says we may not go anywhere. I am upset, but I have to say he deserves to be grounded after what he did.

Last week my parents left Bobby alone at the house while they went out with some friends. Thank heavens I was out shopping with Tammy. While they were gone, my brother had this idea to try and cook some brownies. He knows he's not supposed to use the stove while my parents are gone, but I guess the brownies were calling his name louder than my parents' warnings were.

To make a long story short, Bobby totally destroyed the kitchen. He caught the stove on fire when he was putting butter in the pan. He put the fire out by throwing flour on it and suffocating the flames, but then there was flour all over the counters, the appliances—I mean, everywhere. He decided to try and cleanup some of the mess before my parents got home, so he put the rest of the dishes in the dishwasher. Unfortunately, he grabbed the *dishwashing* liquid instead of the *dishwasher* liquid. When he started the machine, soapsuds went everywhere. The kitchen floor was completely flooded.

I arrived shortly before Mom and Dad and was greeted with bubbles in my face when I opened the back door. Luckily, I had cleared them away enough that I was able to see the expression on Mom and Dad's faces when they walked through the door. I had my camera ready, but they were not amused, so now I am grounded too, but at least I have the picture.

Well, that's all for now. Let me know how things are going in your life. I miss you. Write me back as soon as you can.

Love ya,

Ann Marie

Writing and Sending a Fax

Need to send information in a hurry? Need a message to arrive ASAP? As long as you know the fax, it's as easy as 1, 2, 3 . . . or 555-6575, or whatever the number is—the fax number that is.

A fax is a regular letter, message, or note that is sent electronically by one fax machine to another fax machine. It is different from a letter mailed through the postal service because the original letter remains with the sender. The fax machine acts as a copier and sends a copy of the message to the number that has been dialed. The downside to these instant messages is you can only send someone a fax if he or she has a fax machine to receive your message.

There is no certain style for a fax message. However, it is considered correct to attach a cover sheet to any fax you send, especially if the fax is going to a place of business. If you simply address your note to Ann, but there are five women named Ann at the office, there is no telling who will receive your letter since most offices only have one or two fax machines that are located at a central spot. If a fax is being sent to someone's home, a cover letter is not needed, but it is acceptable to include one.

Most cover letters contain the following information:

❏ name of the recipient   ❏ the date the fax is sent

❏ fax number of the recipient   ❏ name of company, if needed

❏ name of the sender   ❏ subject

❏ fax number of the sender   ❏ number of pages

Cover Sheet

To: _____

_____

Fax Number: _____

From: _____

Fax Number: _____

Subject: _____

Date: _____

Number of Pages: _____

Writing and Sending a Fax (cont.)

Just the Fax, Ma'am

You are a fax repairperson. You have been called to an office building to repair the fax machine. You are not surprised when you get there and find that a mouse has eaten through the cords of the office equipment. You are surprised when you see a fax that a mouse named Pedro has sent to a cat named Louie who lives in Santa Fe.

Cover Sheet

To: Louie the Cat

Fax Number: 343-1111

From: Pedro the Mouse

Fax Number: 898-3456

Subject: Recent Illness

Date: Jan. 6

Pages to follow: 1

Dear Louie,

I do not have much time, but I am writing to let you know I am seriously ill. I am scared I may pass out before I have time to send this fax. I have eaten something that does not agree with me. I was just munching along and then WHAM! It was like a bolt of electricity charged through my stomach. I tried an antacid, but it didn't help.

If something were to happen to me, please take care of my little sister, Anna.
If you must take her to live with you, please see that none of your friends accidentally eat her.

Let me know if you can help.

Pedro

Writing and Sending a Fax *(cont.)*

Directions: Pretend Louie has received the fax from his friend Pedro. Complete the cover sheet, and then in the space provided write a response from Louie the cat to Pedro the mouse.

Cover Sheet

To: _____

_____

Fax Number: _____

From: _____

Fax Number: _____

Subject: _____

Date: _____

Pages to Follow: _____

Dear Pedro,

Pick Up a Pen Instead of Dialing It In: Reasons to Write

When you study something, it is important to know why you are learning it. The importance of writing letters is not hard to understand if you stop and think about it.

People throughout history wrote lengthy letters, even though there was no such thing as the ballpoint pen. It took time to dip their quills into the bottles of ink and write on paper that was less than smooth and snowy white, and yet history shows us that time and time again people wrote letters. Were they crazy? Nah, but they didn't have the telephone and they didn't have computers, so if they wanted to talk to someone who wasn't around they had to write letters.

Many people today can't see any reason to sit down and write a letter when they can use quicker means of communication such as the telephone, the fax machine, or even beepers. Yet despite all of the new ways to send messages, letter writing has not disappeared from our society. It has survived for hundreds of years and will probably survive for hundreds more.

Directions: List 10 reasons why a person might use the telephone instead of writing a letter. Then list 10 reasons why a person might send a letter instead of using the telephone.

10 Reasons for Using the Telephone

1. _____
2. _____
3. _____
4. _____
5. _____
6. _____
7. _____
8. _____
9. _____
10. _____

10 Reasons for Writing a Letter

1. _____
2. _____
3. _____
4. _____
5. _____
6. _____
7. _____
8. _____
9. _____
10. _____

Who Called? Writing Messages and Getting it Right

Though we live in a high-tech world, there are still instances when messages are given and received without the aid of machines. Consequently, writing messages and memos are one of the most important tasks of writing that a person can do. In fact, it is so important that most secretaries have special pads of paper designed especially for taking messages. Read the following telephone conversation and see for yourself how important it is to listen and write down messages accurately.

Ring. Ring. Ring.

Doug: Hello. Who is this?

Tommy: It's Tommy Taylor. I'm calling for Melissa. Is she there?

Doug: Nope.

Tommy: Oh. Well, then, could you take a message for me?

Doug: Sure.

Tommy: Tell her I'm sorry about the misunderstanding. I don't like Amanda. I was just walking her to chemistry class. That's all. Nothing happened. Tell Melissa I can't wait to see her again.

Doug: Okay. I got it.

Tommy: You're sure? It's really important.

Doug: Yep. I got it.

Knock. Knock. Knock.

Doug: Come in.

Melissa: Doug, were there any messages for me while I was out? I was hoping someone might call.

Doug: There was one. Here's the piece of paper where I wrote it all down.

Melissa: Thanks, Doug. I'll read it in my room.

Ring. Ring. Ring.

Pam: Hello.

Melissa: Pam, it's Melissa. I got the worst message while I was out shopping.

Pam: What? What is it?

Melissa: Tommy called. He said he likes Amanda. He says they have chemistry together.

Pam: Oh no!

Melissa: And he said he can't wait to see her.

Pam: Are you sure that's what the message said?

Melissa: Of course I'm sure. My brother wrote it down. If it's written down, it's got to be right. Right?

This mixed-up message makes it obvious that accurately recording information is vital when taking messages. Here are some helpful hints you can remember when writing down a message.

- ❐ Write the name of the person who is to receive the message.
- ❐ Write the name of the person who is leaving the message.
- ❐ Write the time and date that the person called.
- ❐ Write only the information that is an important part of the message.
- ❐ Try to get a phone number where the person can be reached.
- ❐ Be sure and leave your initials or name somewhere on the message. That way, if the person receiving the message has any questions, he or she will know who to ask for help.

Who Called? Writing Messages and Getting it Right *(cont.)*

Teacher Instructions Page

The following is an activity where students receive hands-on practice in writing messages.

Preparation:

- Divide the class into groups of two people each.

- Make copies of message #1 and message #2.

- Cut the phone messages into individual strips.

- Give each student in the group one phone message. (One person in the group should have message #1, and the other person should have message #2.)

- Photocopy the memo sheets on page 62.

- Cut out the memo sheets and distribute one to each student.

- Each student should then have a phone message and a message sheet.

After you have prepared all the materials and passed out the message sheets and the memo sheets, one person in the group will read his or her phone message to the other person in the group. The person receiving the message will fill out the phone memo sheet. Next, have the other partner read his or her message out loud, and the other person in the group will try to record the correct message. When both students in the group are finished, students will compare their answers to the actual messages given.

Encourage students not to repeat information over and over. Part of taking good messages is being a good listener.

In pairs, have students write a telephone conversation. Next, bring two phones to school and place the unplugged phones at the front of the classroom. Place two chairs side by side at the front of the class and pass out memo sheets to the students. Next, have volunteers go to the front and read their conversation to the class while talking on the telephones. The class should take messages during the phone conversations. You can have students check the clock to get the time for the phone calls. Students will love acting out their conversations for the class. Let them have fun. Tell them they can be from foreign countries and use accents, or they can act like someone older or younger than what they really are.

(**Note:** Be sure and remind students not to say anything in their phone conversations that might be disrespectful or hurtful to others.)

Who Called? Writing Messages and Getting it Right *(cont.)*

Message #1

Speaker #1: Hi. This is Janice Westmont from Capital Industries. I need to speak with Ethan Davis, please.

Speaker #2: I'm sorry, Ethan's not available at the moment.

Speaker #1: Oh, well, then could you give him this message, please? Capital Industries loves the tape he sent us. We want to sign him for a recording contract on Wednesday. He needs to meet me at the studio at 3:30 P.M. Tell him if he has any questions to call me tonight at 555-4378. I should be there for most of the evening.

(**Note:** This call occurred at noon on April 13).

Message #2

Speaker #1: Hello, Bobby. It's Kayla. Is Elizabeth at home?

Speaker #2: No, she's not here. She's gone shopping.

Speaker #1: I really need to leave her a message . . . if you don't mind writing it down.

Speaker #2: I don't mind.

Speaker #1: Great. I need to borrow some of her clothes, and I need her to bring them to school tomorrow for me. I want her blue shorts and her red, white, and green top with the buttons and the rounded collar. I also need her silver earrings and her brown sandals—the ones with the buckles, not the laces. She already has my phone number, but she can't call me because I won't be here tonight.

Speaker #2: Okay, I've got it.

(**Note:** This call occurred at 9:30 A.M. on September 13.)

Who Called? Writing Messages and Getting it Right *(cont.)*

Memo Sheets

Memo

Message for: _____

Message from: _____

Date of call: _____

Time of call: _____

Message: _____

_____

_____

_____

_____

_____

_____

Phone number: _____

Message taken by: _____

Memo

Message for: _____

Message from: _____

Date of call: _____

Time of call: _____

Message: _____

_____

_____

_____

_____

_____

_____

Phone number: _____

Message taken by: _____

Memo

Message for: _____

Message from: _____

Date of call: _____

Time of call: _____

Message: _____

_____

_____

_____

_____

_____

_____

Phone number: _____

Message taken by: _____

Memo

Message for: _____

Message from: _____

Date of call: _____

Time of call: _____

Message: _____

_____

_____

_____

_____

_____

_____

Phone number: _____

Message taken by: _____

Who Called? Writing Messages and Getting it Right *(cont.)*

More Messages

Directions: Read the following situations. Using the memo sheets provided on page 62, write down the information needed for each message. Remember to only write down the information that is essential.

1. Mrs. Preston has reminded the class that graduation practice will be held tomorrow on Friday, October 15. Parents may attend if they wish, but only two guests per student are allowed. Practice will be held on the football field, but guests must first stop by the office for a visitor's pass. In case of rain, practice will be held in the gymnasium. Parents may bring cameras. After the practice, there will be a short reception. Food will be provided by the school. Practice will begin as soon as school is over and will last approximately two hours. Everyone is excited about the upcoming event. The principal is so proud of each and every student. If your parents have any questions, please have them call the school.

2. Your neighbor, Mr. Jackson, stopped by your house. He wants you to tell your parents that he and his wife Marge will be out of town Monday, Tuesday, and Wednesday of next week. He needs your parents to keep an eye on the house while they are gone to the country to visit his relatives. He completely trusts them to take care of everything. He needs his outdoor plants watered; and his dog, Maxwell, needs to be walked daily. Don't worry about feeding Max. His daughter Ann is going to stop by each day and take care of food and water for the dog. If you need to get in touch with them, they can be reached at 789-555-1346. That is the phone number for their cellular phone.

3. Aunt Sue calls and tells you that her VCR is broken. The problem is, tonight is the exciting conclusion of the four-part miniseries entitled *The Song of Ray* on channel 4 at eight o'clock. If you could tape it for her, she would be very appreciative. You tell her you will do it, even though you will not be home that evening and have no idea how to program your family's new VCR. (Your father is the only one who knows the complex formula for how to program the device.) Also, your aunt tells you that she will meet your father at your sister's basketball game at seven o'clock by the north bleachers. She wants him to bring the novel he borrowed. It's called *Hope*, and your aunt would like to loan it to her friend Gwen.

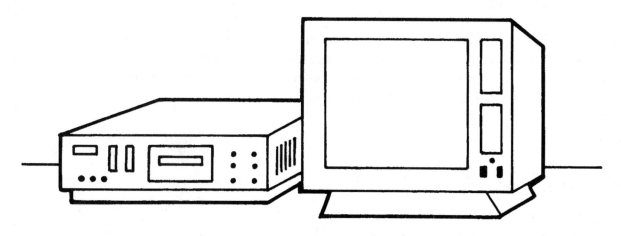

Writing Editorials

You don't agree with these statements? That's okay because you don't have to agree. The statements are simply opinions. An opinion is just one person's thoughts or feelings about a particular subject. An opinion is true to that person but not necessarily true to everyone else.

Editorials in the newspaper are based on opinion. In an editorial, a person can state his or her opinion on just about any topic. An editorial is usually about some issue that many people are familiar with since the writer is trying to evoke some type of reaction from the readers. For example, an editorial about someone's opinion on the migration habits of rare birds of North America would probably not be a very good topic because most people know nothing about the migration habits of the birds nor do they really care. On the other hand, an editorial about capital punishment or abortion would probably evoke a lot of emotion among readers.

Writing an editorial is somewhat different than writing a business letter. When editorials are printed in the newspaper, they do not contain a heading or an inside address. If you actually work for a newspaper, your editorial would not need a salutation, and you would have a by-line instead of a signature. A by-line states who wrote the article. Although the editorial letter is a business letter, paragraphs are indented. Also, no lines are skipped between paragraphs—a newspaper cannot afford to waste space by skipping lines.

People who do not work for the newspaper submit their editorials by writing letters to the editor. The salutation would be to the editor. Most newspapers have a rule that the person writing must sign the letter to the editor or the letter will not be printed. The name of the city where the writer lives is printed underneath the author's name. A person submitting a letter to a newspaper is required to include his full name, phone number, and address; however, the complete address and phone number will not be printed in the paper.

Writing Editorials *(cont.)*

To the Editor:

I am sure anyone that attended the annual Hog Festival this year was as disappointed as I was by the entire organization of the festivities. The Hog Festival is usually something my entire family looks forward to each year. If only we had known how horrible the entire event would be, we could have saved our money and stayed home and rented a movie instead.

First of all, the hogs this year were allowed to run free at the fairgrounds. Although this did allow closer viewing of the animals, it did not allow for easy walking. I had to constantly watch where I stepped. Had I known this would be the case, I can assure you I would not have worn sandals.

The food was also a poor choice. This year, the only meat available to those at the festival was pork. It is extremely hard to eat a bacon, ham, or pork barbecue when the animal in question is staring you in the eye. I feel beef or chicken would have been more appropriate under the circumstances.

Finally, I feel the judging for the beauty pageant was some of the worst I have ever seen. The hog that won slobbered excessively and displayed no real signs of inner beauty. It's my opinion that the entire festival this year was just a bunch of hogwash.

Thelma Lou McKinley
Colliersville

Now it's your turn to give your opinion.

Directions: Think of ten topics you feel strongly about. List the ideas on the lines below. Write your answers in complete sentences.

Example: Students should not have to wear school uniforms.

1. _____

2. _____

3. _____

4. _____

5. _____

6. _____

7. _____

8. _____

9. _____

10. _____

Writing Editorials *(cont.)*

Directions: Choose one of the topics you wrote on page 65. In the space below, write an editorial about the topic you have chosen.

To the Editor:

_____

_____

_____

_____

_____

_____

_____

_____

_____

_____

_____

_____

_____

_____

_____

_____

_____

_____

_____

Writing Editorials *(cont.)*

Sample Lesson Page

To the Editor:

Our county recently proposed the idea of having year-round school for our school system. The committee gathered evidence showing the benefits of year-round school. They claimed tax dollars would be better spent if the buildings were not left empty for eight weeks during the summer. They also claimed students' retention of information would be higher and test scores would improve. Anyone with a grain of sense would realize this idea is simply ridiculous.

Students need a break. Teachers and students would experience severe burnout if school stayed in session all year. Learning would decrease rather than increase. Furthermore, anyone who has ever been to a school building in the summer realizes the building does not sit empty. Community theater, sports, clubs, and special classes all meet in the so-called empty building during the summer hours.

Finally, I find it interesting that the reports never mention students' opinions on the proposed idea. If you are trying to help students, why not consult them? It just makes good sense.

Cameron Saunders
Glendale

Saying It with Pictures: The Editorial Cartoon

You've probably heard the saying, a picture's worth a thousand words. If only your English teacher believed this you wouldn't mind those long papers you have to do. You could just draw them instead of writing them. (Hey, it doesn't hurt to dream a little.)

You may never get to draw your final exam or your five-page essay, but there is one place where a picture can be used in place of a thousand words, and that's the editorial cartoon.

The editorial cartoon is much like the editorial. All editorials are based on someone's opinion—the reader may agree or disagree with the writer's viewpoint. An editorial cartoon will deal with an issue with which many people are familiar. Editorial cartoons are designed to make the reader stop and think about a particular issue. To study examples of editorial cartoons, look at several newspapers. Both daily and weekly papers usually contain at least one editorial cartoon in each issue of the paper.

❏ Remember that an editorial cartoon may not be funny to everyone.

❏ An editorial cartoon deals with issues that are well known to most of the subscribers of the paper.

❏ The message is as important as the illustration.

❏ Some editorial cartoons do not require any written information. The cartoon is the message.

Saying It with Pictures:
The Editorial Cartoon *(cont.)*

Directions: Look at the two editorial cartoons below. On the lines provided, write a caption for each.

_____

_____

_____

_____

_____

_____

In the frame below, design your own editorial cartoon and caption.

Writing to Get Advice

Sometimes people need advice. One way to receive advice is to write a letter to someone who writes an advice column. Most newspapers print letters from people seeking advice. The columnist will respond to the letters by offering his or her opinion on the topic. When writing to a newspaper, the writer will usually include his or her name and address with the original letter. However, if the newspaper prints the letter, they may opt to omit the writer's real name.

Dear Gabby:

I need your help. My best friend always wants to copy my homework. She says it's not her fault that she doesn't get the work finished. She blames her basketball coach for keeping the entire team at practice until late at night. Since they practice four nights a week and have games two nights a week, my friend never has her work done.

I know it's cheating to let her copy the assignment from me, but I don't know what else to do. She is the best friend I've ever had, and I don't want to lose her friendship. Do you have any advice for me?

Signed,
Hopelessly Mixed Up!

Dear Hopelessly Mixed Up:

You're the loser in this game. Tell your friend to get her work done or to find someone else to play with!

Signed,
Gabby

Remember the following when writing letters:

❏ Begin your letter with the greeting.

❏ Place a comma after the greeting.

❏ Indent paragraphs.

❏ Place a comma after the closing.

Writing to Get Advice *(cont.)*

Part 1

Directions: On the lines provided, list 10 problems where you might need to seek advice. The problems can be silly or serious, real or imaginary.

Example: Your cat, Moochie, has a best friend who's a mouse.

1. _____
2. _____
3. _____
4. _____
5. _____
6. _____
7. _____
8. _____
9. _____
10. _____

Part 2

Directions: Choose one of the problems listed above. In the space below, write a letter to an advice columnist. When you are finished, swap letters with someone in the classroom and write a response to his or her letter.

Dear _____,

_____

_____

_____

_____

_____

_____

Signed,

_____

A Lime-Colored Sofa With Broken Springs: Writing for the Classifieds

---

For Sale

One lime-colored sofa with broken springs. Needs cleaning. It's old but it's cheap. Call 555-4343 and make an offer.
I guarantee you there's not another sofa like this one.

Does the advertisement above make you want to rush out and buy the sofa? Look at the advertisement below and see if it sounds better.

For Sale

Green sofa with extra-soft seating. Needs some tender loving care. This antique is a rare find! Call 555-4343 if you're interested in this one-of-a-kind deal.

Good writers know that word choice is essential. Positive words are usually better than negative words, (unless you're trying to write a horror story or some other type of work that requires negative images).

Part 1

Directions: Look at the following list of words. Change each word or phrase so that it still has the same meaning but sounds more positive.

Examples: old—<u>antique</u>   Smelly odor—<u>Unique scent</u>

1. short   _____

2. fat   _____

3. slightly stained   _____

4. in need of repair   _____

5. lazy   _____

6. skinny   _____

7. crowded location   _____

8. someone who lies   _____

9. bald   _____

10. stubborn   _____

Part 2

Directions: Look at the following picture. On the back of this sheet, write an advertisement to help sell the item. Remember, use only positive words.

Writing and Following Instructions

Teacher Instructions Page

Getting students to understand the importance of following instructions is not always an easy task, but it is definitely worth the effort. What's the best way to teach such an important skill? To teach this lesson it may simply be better to show than to tell.

Preparaton:

- Bring a jacket or coat to class.

- Make copies of the worksheets on pages 74 and 75.

- Pass out copies of the worksheet on page 74; read the material on this page to the class.

- Pass out copies of the worksheet on page 75.

- Follow the directions given for Section A of Part 2 on page 75.

When everyone has finished writing instructions for how to put on a jacket, ask for a volunteer to read his or her paper out loud. As the student reads his instructions, try to put on the jacket.

The task will be nearly impossible because most students do not even begin with the most basic instruction: pick up the jacket. It is hard to put on something that is not in your hands.

After two or three students have read their instructions, discuss what changes are needed for the instructions to be correct.

Now tell the students to work on Section B of the worksheet and to write instructions, for sharpening a pencil. When everyone has finished, ask for a volunteer to go to the pencil sharpener. Next, have someone read his or her instructions. Instructions this time should be more accurate as students should begin to understand the importance of detail when writing directions. Be sure and point out that following and listening to instructions is as important as giving good instructions. Even a good explanation will not work if the other person doesn't pay attention to the details.

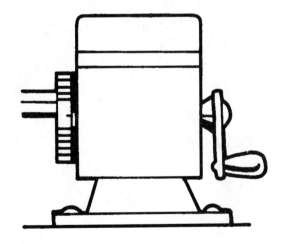

Writing and Following Instructions *(cont.)*

Part 1

Read the following conversation between a teacher and a student:

Teacher: Write your name in the upper right-hand corner of your paper and then place your paper in the basket.

Student: Where do I write my name again?

Teacher: The same place you've written it every day, all year long.

Student: Do I have to write my last name, too?

Teacher: If your last name is Slammerkowinjowskinovinski, then no. Everyone else, yes.

Student: Where did you say to write our names again?

Teacher: In the upper right-hand corner. No, that's the left-hand corner.

Student: I can't find my pencil. Do you have one I can borrow?

Teacher: I'm not a bookstore.

Student: Well, I don't see how you expect me to write my name without a pencil.

Teacher: Just write your name in the upper right-hand corner of your paper!

Student: I don't have a pencil. This isn't fair!

Teacher: Fair is where you go to get a ribbon for your hog.

Student: Did she just call me a hog?

Teacher: Please give me strength.

Student: Was that the bell? I know what that means. Hey, what is it I'm supposed to do with this paper?

Teacher: Everyone should learn how to give and follow directions.

Some helpful hints on giving instructions or directions are as follows:

- Keep the instructions simple.
- Tell or write the instructions in a specific order.
- Use visuals when needed.
- Go back over the instructions for clarity.

The best way to follow directions is by learning to listen. Follow the instructions exactly as they are given. How do you accomplish this? Practice. Practice. Practice.

Writing and Following Instructions *(cont.)*

Part 2

Section A

Directions: Imagine your friend from the Bahamas has never before worn a coat. He is about to go on a cruise to Alaska, so he will need to wear one when he goes on his trip.

In the space provided, write directions to your friend so he will know how to put on his new coat.

Note: Work on Section A only. Do not complete Section B until your teacher asks you to begin.

```
Instructions for How to Put on a Coat




```

Section B

Directions: Your best friend always uses a mechanical pencil, but she is out of lead, and she had to purchase a nonmechanical pencil from the bookstore to use during math class. There's only one small problem: your friend doesn't know how use the pencil sharpener.

In the space provided, write instructions for your friend on how to use the pencil sharpener.

```
Instructions for Using a Pencil Sharpener




```

To Be or Knot to Be: That is the Question!

You are the manager of the Foot Palace Shoe Store. Your store specializes in shoes with laces. There are no shoes in your store with buckles or Velcro, only laces.

Because you're the only store in the area that sells the new supersonic, flight-simulating, blue-and-white-striped leather tennis shoe, your store is overwhelmed with customers. You've had to hire extra help, and fast. Business is booming. Sales are increasing. Life is wonderful.

There's only one little problem:

Not a single shoe that comes into your store is ever laced. Every new pair is just lying there with the laces in the box. Five empty holes on both sides of each shoe's tongue sit empty and waiting to be laced.

It seemed simple enough: hire people to lace the shoes; sell the shoes; make lots of money. Only one small problem: no one seems to remember how to lace the shoes. One salesperson even asked if there was supposed to be a knot or not! You are at your wit's end.

Thank heavens you took a class on how to write directions. Now all you have to do is write down for your employees a simple little chart that tells them how to lace the shoes and where to start. Don't forget these important rules when writing directions:

- Use short, simple sentences.

- Write instructions in the order the task should be completed.

- Use visuals when needed.

- Be specific.

- Avoid confusing terms or words.

- Try out the directions you've written to see if any part is confusing or unclear.

Here is a picture of your super-selling sneaker with the laces in the shoe:

Directions: On a separate piece of paper, write the steps needed to help someone lace a tennis shoe. Refer to the picture above as needed. Use pictures in your directions only to help explain a written step. Do not use pictures in place of written information.

Seeing is Believing: Writing Directions

Have you ever had someone write down directions for you, but the directions didn't really make any sense? Sometimes a map or a drawing can help clear up confusing directions. The minute you see the picture, you begin to understand the words. Some people learn better by seeing how something is done rather than simply hearing or reading about it. The same is true with directions. Whether directions are written or drawn, the rules for giving directions are similar.

- Keep the directions simple.

- Write/draw neatly.

- Be specific.

- Don't give more information than what is needed.

Here is a sample of a map and its corresponding set of directions:

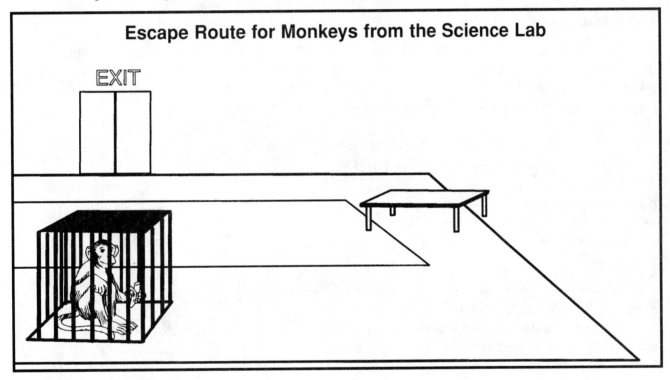

Escape Route for Monkeys from the Science Lab

EXIT

Directions:

1. Monkeys will exit through cage door.
2. Go straight down the path.
3. Turn left at the end of the path.
4. Go straight.
5. Crawl under lab table.
6. Continue straight.
7. Turn left at the end of the path.
8. Exit through doors on the right of the path.

By seeing the map and reading the directions, it is clear which route the monkeys will have to take to escape the science lab.

Directions: On a separate sheet of paper, draw a map from your house to the school. Then write directions explaining how to get from your house to the school.

It's Everywhere! It's Everywhere!
Writing Is all Around You

Writing is a part of our everyday world. Before most people are even fully awake they've already seen writing on their tube of toothpaste or on their box of breakfast donuts. Writing is all around you.

Materials:

- packages/labels/boxes with writing on them
- classroom set of "Package That Product" (below)

Preparation: Divide students into groups of four. Give each group at least five different packages to examine. Have students read over the written information and then compile a list of similarities among the different products.

Students will likely discover that although the words are different, most contain the same types of information (for example, information about where the product was made, who made the product, ingredients or materials lists, etc.).

Next, have students look through the items they've brought with them to class. Excluding obvious items such as textbooks and notebooks, have them list things that have writing on them. Have each group share the lists with the rest of the class. After discussing the results, complete the rest of this page.

Package That Product

The next time you go to the grocery store stop at the cereal aisle and take a look. Don't stay there too long, or people will think it is a little strange; but while you're there, pick up a box or two of cereal. There is more writing on one box of cereal than in some chapters of your schoolbooks.

Someone writes all the words that go on a cereal box. Someone writes the words for the advertisements that sell everything that can be sold. Someone is determined to get you to pick Mr. Munchies over someone else's Mrs. Good-i-os. Someone is doing a tremendous amount of writing. Writing is everywhere.

Directions: Imagine you have invented a yo-yo that walks the dog. No, it really walks the dog. Now family and friends can enjoy their yo-yo's while taking the pooch out for exercise.

On another sheet of paper, design the packaging for your new product. Give the product a name and include any important information that is needed by the consumer.

Answer Key

Page 27

The Six Parts of the Business Letter:

1. Heading
2. Inside Address
3. Salutation or Greeting
4. Body
5. Closing
6. Signature

The Five Parts of the Friendly Letter:

1. Heading
2. Inside Address
3. Salutation or Greeting
4. Body
5. Closing
6. Signature

Page 31

Answers will vary. Possibilities include the following:

1. You were unhappy with your service at a restaurant.
2. The clothes you bought shrunk the first time you washed them.
3. You found a hair in the ice cream sundae you bought at the ice cream parlor.
4. Your cable keeps cutting off.
5. Your new video game is nothing like the commercial claimed.
6. The cafeteria keeps serving spinach and liver.
7. Your summer employer refuses to write you your final paycheck.
8. The fish you bought at the pet store died in less than twenty-four hours.
9. Your favorite frozen pizza is no longer being made.
10. You had a perm put in your hair, and your hair became straight instead of curly.

Page 40

1. signature
2. state
3. self-addressed, stamped envelope
4. cc
5. enclosure
6. SAE
7. notation
8. self-addressed,
9. P.O. (or post office)
10. enc.
11. Minnesota
12. NC

Page 42

Wendy Britt
21 Davis Street
Nashville, TN 35671-0276

Ann Crede
700 Robin Lane
Carrington, NV 67439-1243

(**Note:** State names may be spelled out completely or abbreviated. Either way is correct.)

Page 48

Accept reasonable answers.

Page 57

To: Pedro the Mouse
Fax Number: 898-3456
From: Louie the Cat
Fax Number: 343-1111
Subject: (Answers will vary.)
Date: (Answers will vary.)
Pages to Follow: (Answers will vary.)

Page 58

Accept reasonable answers. Possibilities include the following:

10 Reasons for Using the Telephone

1. to get an immediate response to a question
2. to see if someone is at home
3. to order flowers, etc. when you need something ordered on a particular day
4. to talk to a friend and get an immediate response
5. to have a friend help you study or do homework
6. to call for emergency help
7. to talk to a small child who is unable to read or write letters
8. to try and win a contest from a radio station
9. to make reservations for dinner
10. to call and see what time a movie, etc. begins

Answer Key *(cont.)*

Page 58 *(cont)*

10 Reasons for Writing a Letter

1. to enclose money for an order
2. to apply for a job
3. to have contact with someone who is rarely home
4. to let someone know how you feel if you are too shy to say it
5. to send holiday greetings
6. to enclose legal documents or items which require a signature
7. to send an invitation with directions enclosed
8. to send pictures to someone who lives far away and enclose a special message about the photographs
9. to give the person something special he or she can read over and over again
10. to have a pen pal

Page 61

Message #1

Message for: Ethan Davis

Message from: Janice Westmont

Date & time of call: April 13, 12:00 P.M.

Message: Capital Industries is interested in Ethan signing a contract. Be at the studio Wednesday at 3:30 P.M. May call with questions.

Phone number: 555-4378

Signed: (Answers will vary.)

Message #2

Message for: Elizabeth

Message from: Kayla

Date & time of call: September 13, 9:30 A.M.

Message: Kayla needs to borrow blue shorts; red, white and green top with the buttons and rounded collar; silver earrings; and brown sandals with the buckles. Bring them to school tomorrow.

Phone number: She won't be home to receive a call.

Signed: (Answers will vary.)

Page 63

Message #1

Message To: your parents

Message From: Mrs. Preston

Date: Thursday, October 14

Message: Graduation practice is Friday, October 15. Parents may attend. Two guests per student. Practice is on the football field. If it rains, we'll practice in the gym. Get a visitor's pass upon entering the building. Cameras are allowed. A reception will immediately follow. Food provided by the school. Practice starts after school and lasts two hours. Any questions, call the school.

Your Name: (Answers will vary.)

Message #2

Message To: your parents

Message From: Mr. Jackson

Date: (Answers will vary.)

Message: Mr. Jackson needs you to watch his house Monday, Tuesday, and Wednesday of next week. Outdoor plants need watering. Maxwell needs to be walked each day, but he doesn't need food or water Any questions, call 789-555-1346.

Your Name: (Answers will vary.)

Message #3

Message To: your father

Message From: Aunt Sue

Date: (Answers will vary.)

Message: Tape "The Song of Ray" on channel 4 at 8:00 tonight. Also, Aunt Sue will meet you for the baskeball game at 7:00 by the north bleachers. Bring the novel called *Hope*.

Page 72

Accept reasonable answers. Possibilities include the following:

1. petite, vertically challenged
2. healthy looking
3. unusually colored
4. a handyman's dream
5. ready to be motivated
6. slender
7. metropolitan, urban growth
8. a teller of tales, a quick thinker
9. well groomed
10. strong-willed